REMAKING ACHILLES

WINNER OF THE
Willow Run Poetry Book Award

Hidden River Arts offers the Willow Run Poetry Book Award for an unpublished collection of poetry, in English, of 75 to 100 pages. The award provides $1000 and publication by Hidden River Publishing on its Hidden River Press imprint.

Hidden River Arts is an interdisciplinary arts organization dedicated to supporting and celebrating the unserved artists among us, particularly those outside the artistic and academic mainstream.

REMAKING ACHILLES

Slicing into Angola's History

CAROL TYX

HIDDEN RIVER PRESS

Philadelphia   2020

Cover design by Cheryl Totty
Interior design and typography by P. M. Gordon Associates

Library of Congress Control Number: 2020930451
ISBN 978-0-9994915-2-2

HIDDEN RIVER PRESS
An imprint of Hidden River Publishing
Philadelphia, Pennsylvania

for the readers in the
Anamosa State Penitentiary Book Club

CONTENTS

REMAKING ACHILLES
FEBRUARY, 1951

INSIDE THE BIG HOUSE: THE CITIZEN COMMITTEE INVESTIGATION
FEBRUARY TO APRIL, 1951

AFTERMATH: AIN'T OVER YET
BEYOND APRIL, 1951

INTRODUCTION

BEFORE 2008, I HAD NEVER seen a prison from the inside. Prison seemed like a foreign country, one I was not particularly interested in visiting. All that changed in the years my colleague Mary Vermillion and I facilitated a book club at Anamosa State Penitentiary with students from our small college in Iowa. While the media had taught us that inmates would be callous and cruel, our Anamosa partners were smart, thoughtful, and reflective.

As part of doing research for an article Mary and I were writing about the Prison Book Club, I read Wilbert Rideau's memoir, *In the Place of Justice*. As Rideau described his first days at Angola in the 1960s, he commented that the prison budget had just been slashed, and Rideau feared "that the reforms gained in the 1950s after 31 white prisoners slashed their Achilles tendons to protest conditions at Angola would be lost" (36). Rideau went on to recount the horrific conditions at Angola in the sixties and seventies, but I was transfixed by that one sentence: 31 men had slashed their own heels. It seemed surreal to me.

That single detail haunted me, and eventually I visited Angola in the summer of 2015 to see for myself the site of what became known as the Heel-String incident. Retired criminal justice professor and Angola historian Marianne Fisher-Giorlando graciously shared many of her personal newspaper clippings about the Heel-Stringers and helped facilitate a tour that included a visit to the Red Hat cell block, now an Historic Landmark, and the remains of Camp H, one of the prison camps at the time of the Heel-Stringers.

The 1951 Heel-String incident has its roots in Angola's history. Beginning in 1844, the state of Louisiana began leasing prisoners, at first to do contract labor within the Baton Rouge penitentiary. In 1869 the lease went to Samuel James. With virtually no accountability, James sub-leased prisoners to live and work outside the penitentiary. They built and maintained roads and levees and worked in the fields on former plantations, including James' Angola plantation. Inmates were housed in old sharecropper buildings, which eventually became Camp A, where African American prisoners lived out their sentences. In many ways leasing was both a continuation of slavery and an early model of the privatized, for-profit prison. Eventually the state of Louisiana, realizing the profit to be made on prison labor, purchased Angola and ended the leasing system in 1901.

While the treatment of inmates varied in the first half of the twentieth century depending on who held positions of authority, a number of factors led to deplorable living conditions. The state pushed the prison to be self-sustaining, with minimal funds for infrastructure. Inmates, living in racially segregated camps spread around the 18,000 acre farm, stayed in barracks-type housing, with as many as 300 men in one barrack.

In order to cut costs, inmates served as armed "trustee" guards. Inmates practically ran the prison. Besides acting as guards, they managed the kitchens, kept the books, and built any new facilities. Education and rehabilitation were not considerations. The goal was to make a profit, or at least make the prison pay for itself. This encouraged field guards to use harsh measures, including flogging with a leather strap known as "The Bat" or beating with hickory sticks. Until just before the Heel-String incident, stocks were still a form of punishment. In the 1940s, the Department of Justice made two official investigations and their reports strongly indicted living conditions and the treatment of inmates. Neither of these resulted in substantial reforms.

All of this history provided the build-up to what became known as the Heel-String incident. The protest started when seven men from Camp E, which housed "uncooperative" white offenders, slashed the Achilles tendon of their left leg. All of the original Heel-Stringers had been part of a thirteen-man escape attempt. Fearing retaliation, the men disabled themselves so they could not perform field work, the site of most killings. The Heel-String seven sent out a call to widen the protest and thirty-one men, all white, became Heel-Stringers, joined later by 6 more men from Camp H. The original thirty-one were treated initially by the only medical personnel on site, Nurse Mary Margaret Daughtry. The incident was not reported to the public until an anonymous letter arrived at the *Shreveport Journal* several weeks later. From that point on, local news media played an important role in keeping pressure on the prison system.

Superintendent Rollo Lawrence and Warden Ralph Easterly insisted that allegations of brutality at Angola were unfounded. Under public pressure, Governor Earl Long selected thirty-four citizens to investigate the incident and make recommendations. Presumably to get the media off his back, fourteen of the committee members were journalists, including Dolph Frantz, editor of the *Shreveport Journal*, who chaired the committee, and vice-chair Maggie Dixon, editor of the Baton Rouge *Morning Advocate*.

The citizen committee, charged with completing their work in sixty days, worked diligently between the end of February and mid-April, 1951, holding interviews both on and off site with prisoners, prison employees, and administrators. While the initial interviews led to conflicting testimony, over time a clearer picture of conditions at Angola emerged. The committee made twenty recommendations, many of them echoing the Department of Justice reports from the previous decade, but this time the criticism was coming not from the outside, but from Louisiana's own citizens.

Still, there was resistance to change. While Governor Earl Long and Warden Easterly made minor adjustments, the major issues were not addressed under Governor Long's tenure. Judge Robert Kennon, running in the 1952 governor's race on a platform that included improving conditions at Angola, beat Long's hand-picked successor.

By focusing on this incident that involved white prisoners, I do not mean to imply that white men at Angola lived under more deplorable conditions than black men. The infamous "dungeons"—concrete boxes buried underground to punish with sensory deprivation—were built in Camp A, which housed African American prisoners. Angola mirrored the outside world of the 1950s in its structures of segregation, and ever since the official end of slavery in the United States, prisons had become one of the tools of re-enslavement. The 1951 Easter Uprising in Camp A, which became the subject of a number of poems, reveals the oppressive conditions for African American men at Angola. Today the United States incarcerates its citizens with the highest rate in the world, with that rate riding heavily on the bodies of African American men. As Michelle Alexander powerfully argues in *The New Jim Crow*, mass incarceration operates as a system of racialized social control. Angola is part of this system.

While the poems that follow are a work of the imagination, they are strongly informed by accounts written by local reporters. Their commitment to probing the Heel-String incident led to substantial reforms at Angola, and while many of the reforms did not endure, they became part of the long saga of transforming "the worst prison in the nation" to a place that is doing cutting edge work on reducing recidivism today. Yet in a state with exceedingly high incarceration rates and harsh sentencing laws, much remains to be transformed.

LONG AND WINDING ROAD

Once you could only get there by boat.
Now there's a narrow road through the tangle
of the Tunica Hills, no shoulder,
dead ending at the gate.

From the turnoff onto LA 66 a sprinkle of trailers,
a post office, an elementary school, three churches—
two Baptist, one Methodist—a sign that reads
Jesus Christ is Lord of Tunica, then nothing

but trees and a descending, as if you were
winding through Dante's circles until you hit bottom—
The Farm, The Big House, Alcatraz of the South,
Siberia of Dixie—Angola.

THE LEASED OF THESE

1844–1901

FIRST HEEL-SLASHER: THEOPHILE CHEVALIER

He stole five dollars, perhaps to purchase
a pair of shoes. For taking that five
he got five years.

Leased as a convict to S.L. James
he worked outside without shoes
the winter of 1885–86

the year sparrows froze in record numbers
and in the muck of building a levee, his toes numb
he lost his balance and was beaten.

He learned to center himself
on his heels, his feet turning gray
then a waxy black.

When he couldn't walk anymore
someone slashed his foot off
with a penknife.

A week later the other foot
fell off. Theophile Chevalier
kept working.

The Leased of These

THE LEASED OF THESE

*And the King will answer them, "Truly, I say to you, as you
did it to one of the least of these my brothers, you did it to me."*
—Matthew 25:40

For sixty years, prisoners were leased
at first for nothing, so the state would not have to feed
and shelter them, later for a rental fee
sometimes paid, sometimes not.

As the leased, they built levees and railroads
chopped cotton, cut cane. As the leased
they had a life expectancy of six years.
The *Daily Picayune* editor thought the death penalty
would be more humane.

Those in favor of the system worried that to end leasing
would take resources away from others who were the least—
the blind, the sick, the insane. Sometimes the leased
were the same, but convicts worked—
it was the least they could do.

LEASEE: S.L. JAMES

As a civil engineer, I knew how to manage—
prisoners were just another project.
Twenty-five years I organized cheap, dependable labor
not just for my plantation—Angola—
but for my friends and neighbors.

I wanted to be part of making Louisiana
great, providing muscle for railroads
and levees, creating an agrarian empire.
I never had any trouble, although one year
I lost over two hundred. It seemed only fair
to skip the lease fee that year.

More than once the legislature tried
to push against me, but I knew how to
grease the wheels. My eulogist got it right:
A singularly sagacious man of business,
eminently successful in all that he undertook.

My executors divvied up
over two million dollars.

HOW TO MAKE A PLANTATION PRISON

after Frank X Walker

Buy a plantation,
preferably a big one in a remote location.

House convicts in the slave quarters.
When the quarters collapse, build the convict camp on the same site.

Make sure most prisoners are black.
Make sure all prisoners know they are expendable.

When more than a hundred prisoners die in a year,
increase arrests.

Raise cotton. Pick it by hand.
Or substitute sugar for cotton. Cut that by hand, too.

Keep profits high by slashing wages to almost nothing
or better yet, eliminate them.

Make twelve-hour days the norm.
Use flogging to combat exhaustion.

Spend as little as possible on medical care,
nothing on education.

Hire prisoners as overseers. Give them guns and no pay.
When there's a shooting, don't ask questions.

THE LONG LINE

1901–1951

LONG LINE

Ain't got what it takes for the long line today
four miles out, four miles back, fall in before dawn
back by dinner if you lucky, after dark if you not

Scramble for your hoe, dull as the day
if you can't keep up, get whipped
seasons change, wardens change, the long line stays

Feel the blisters comin' on, no socks, no tryin' on shoes for fit
slow down, the bat find you, take you off the field flat
better to go down swinging that hoe even if the sun done burnt you up

Long line never get shorter, world without end, amen

BEFORE I WAS ACHILLES I

Before I was Achilles I was a DOC number
and before that I was that faggot from Lafayette
who enlisted to see if I could make myself a man but I come out
with the same eye for hard flesh. First day at The Farm
I watch the man beside me, how he flex that arm—whack, whack—
stalks falling everywhere. I jump in, grab and slash,
blood running with the juice, leaves sharper than my machete.
I step back, look again, admire the firmness of that man's muscle.
Guard yank me out the line, you bastard, you at Angola,
you gonna work. I try to tell him I never cut cane,
but he's already yelling for the Captain.

Take me back to camp, tie me to a post
pour castor oil down my throat, taste like tar.
Feel like somebody stomping all over my insides.
Then out it come, down my legs, pooling 'round my heels.
I'm ready to scream but my breath stops
like there's nothing inside me at all.
Everybody back away. I see that guard smirking
and I think someday I'm gonna kill somebody.

Lady in white walk by, look me in the eye
'fore she put her hand over her nose.
Leadbelly song keep circling my head—
Take a Whiff on Me.

IT BAD ENOUGH

It bad enough to wear these damned stripes
but why couldn't they give us underwear—
laundry once a week and half the time no toilet paper—
you add it up.

I tell Nurse Daughtry it stink like
the hold of a slaveship. She white
but she get it, remembered what I said,
told that investigation.

Only this ship ain't goin' nowhere.
We locked in this hold year after year,
only the dead escape that smell.

FIFTIES PHOTO

You might think you were in Poland
a decade earlier—the triple tiers
the striped suits, the ill-fitting shoes
the listless bodies hunched, hanging over
the stacked plank beds, the frozen faces
onyx eyes staring
straight at you.

FOUND POEM 1: DEPARTMENT OF JUSTICE SURVEY AND RECOMMENDATIONS, STATE OF LOUISIANA PENITENTIARY SYSTEM, 1945/1948

Buildings in state of obsolescence and dilapidation . . . many in such a state of repair as to be entirely unsuited for further use of any kind . . . fire hazard grave . . . Hospital at Camp H could be salvaged as a cattle barn . . . appalling condition of laundry and culinary services . . . unhealthy and inadequate water and sewage systems . . . sanitary facilities practically useless . . . educational facilities practically non-existent.

MAIL NOTES

Mail night once a week.
Yardman call your name, you not there,
maybe on a late crew, mail get tossed
or maybe you there and yardman
hungry, want to go home, last letters pitched.

One time I found a hundred letters
back of an old desk, money orders, too.
More mail than I ever got in fourteen years.
I play Yardman, pass out letters for a nickel.

GREENS

An order for greens from some Chicago firm
in February, the Mississippi breaching the levees
spinach two feet under.

All day we stand in cold water
reach into brown swirl
find them slippery leaves

bat ready to strike if we pause—
all that green ready to harvest
for somebody's pocket.

LEVEE LIFE OF MAGGIE DIXON

Long before I co-chaired the investigation committee
I had a heart for the inmates at Angola.
These were the men of my childhood
levee builders who hauled dirt for my grandfather
and after he died, my father, and after he died,
my stepfather, all engineers who spent their lives
trying to keep the Big Muddy in line.

Until I went to high school our home was a tent
near a steamboat landing. Roger and Corrine went off
to boarding school, but I stayed to care for my stepsisters.
I didn't mind. I love the backwaters of Louisiana, the smell
of murky water, the fishiness, the late afternoon light
when the men return to camp like sea creatures
crawling onto land, their mud-streaked faces glistening.
Sometimes at night I heard them singing, sparks of light
rippling over the dark water.

JOHN BLUE

Escapee John Blue, red-hatted,
over sixty, sent back to the fields
after his recapture in Quincy, Illinois
months after he disappeared
into the Tunica Hills.
Two days of humid heat—
sunstroke.

Captain, Camp E:
A allus waz unlucky that way!
The old so-and-so ups and dies on me
before I git a chance to kill him!
An' I only got to put the bat on him jist once!

POST MORTEM: JOHN BLUE

After heat took out John Blue—
three more next day—
every foreman got a thermometer.
We too hot, supposed to rest.

Old Marse break out the mercury
so we never be too hot—
don't stop men dying.

Them thermometers die off, too.
Rumor be they can't read them anyway.

FOUND POEM 2: DEPARTMENT OF JUSTICE SURVEY AND RECOMMENDATIONS, STATE OF LOUISIANA PENITENTIARY SYSTEM, 1945/1948

Irresponsible, irreformable inmates convicted of offenses involving
the use of violence handle and control practically all firearms
available on the penitentiary grounds . . . supervision and training
of inmate farm workers is under armed prisoners most of who stand
convicted of serious charges involving the use of the very weapons
they are entrusted with . . . disband convict guard force as soon as
possible.

CONVICT GUARDS

Murderers preferred
or rapists

Negroes often sought for this position
used to taking orders

Average IQ white guard: 84
Average IQ Negro counterpart: 69.5

In charge of count
often the only guard at night

Two dollars a month
payable only at discharge

Unpaid if demoted
or killed

PELICAN CANNERY

Every day I load a thousand cans
stamped "made in Baton Rouge"—
Baton Rouge fifty-five miles away.

No inspector ever come
and no Angola free people
eat food from the Pelican Cannery.

We get the vegetables
too rotten to be canned.

SPOON

I'm a prized possession
a hot item, so sleep with me
keep me close
while you work.

Put me in your mouth, baby
spoon that watery stew in
those green tomatoes
rejected by the cannery
those soggy field peas.

If you can't afford the nickel
eat with your fingers,
keep me in your pocket, baby
hold me tight.

PRISON CAPTAIN

Yes, I flogged a prisoner today—
the man who cooks for my family—
makes a rump roast my wife say the best
she ever taste, a sweet potato pie to die for.

Today I roast his rump, took all my strength
to give him what he deserve
and even then I wore out before I finished
had to get my cousin next door to help me out
'til I could finish the job.

My daughter, she love that sweet potato pie, too.
I just come in from my shift
and I seen her in the kitchen sneaking a piece
before supper and that nigger brush her hand
givin' her a slice. Couldn't get that strap fast enough—
smack that coon back to the field.

Yeah, it happened one time before.
Why didn't I ask for him to be removed?
Well, he shouldn't have done it
and his pie so good.

REMAKING ACHILLES

FEBRUARY, 1951

REMAKING ACHILLES: THE HEEL-SLASHERS

These thirty-one men had no hope
of immortality. After crossing
into the underworld of Angola
they sought to live only long enough
to return to the free world
and so for them the razor arrow,
crippling as it might be, held the hope
of mortality, the chance to live before dying.

If they couldn't walk
they couldn't work in the fields,
and if they couldn't work in the fields
they wouldn't have to confront the convict guards
who towered above them on horseback
and carried guns. And so they passed the dull blade
from man to man in Camp E, the strongest tendon
in the body snapping like a windowshade.

They did not flinch as they hobbled
to the hospital in Camp H
dragging their disconnected feet,
praying this would be the heel
that would save them.

LINEAGE

The Heel-Slashers, who did not have access
to a library, did not know
they were following the footsteps
of Flemish anatomist Philip Verheyen
who discovered the Achilles tendon
by dissecting his own leg.

HEEL STREET BOOGIE

Tommy Sargent and the Range Boys picking
Steel Guitar Boogie ain't got nothin' on us.

We boogying between the beds
like we on Louisiana Hayride, hopping

on our one good leg, sliding on the strings
we got left. We a hillbilly band now, no more

long line for us, we got other lines to sing—
we infectious, gonna cripple this entire operation.

We may limp, but we alive—Heel Street Boogie
all night long.

FIRST RESPONDER: NURSE DAUGHTRY

They shuffled to the hospital in Camp H
one foot dragging behind the other.
The warden, the sheriff, the patients—
they all turned to me.

What was I to do?
I wanted to be a doctor, but that world
wasn't for women in my day
so I became a nurse, and here they came
limping down the hall, a broken line.

We couldn't wait the hours it would take
to get a doctor here. I had worked in surgery
five years at Baton Rouge General
so I got out the sutures and stitched
those tendons together.

Later, talking to the reporters, Dr. Littell
who had only worked at Angola a few days
had the nerve to claim *I don't think they have
any justification for all this business.*

I didn't need those boys to tell me why they did it.
I had been in every camp in my seven and a half years
behind the big gate. I knew what it meant.

DR. I.F. LITTELL TAKES A WALK AROUND THE BLOCK

I was truthful when I told the reporters
I had seen no evidence of beatings or brutality
and when the newspaper quoted me as saying
I don't think they have any justification
for all this business, I was not part of a cover-up.

I had only worked sporadically at Angola,
a day here and there for a couple months,
and every wound I stitched up, came from
one inmate stabbing another, I was told.

In the days to come, as I read accounts
in the same newspaper where I denied
any mistreatment, I would come to question
my own testimony.

TUNNEL-DIGGER TO HEEL-STRINGER: WALLACE MACDONALD

We weren't in this to reform the prison—
we were in this to save our lives.
Us tunnel-diggers had been caught and
we had word: our days were numbered.
It would be easy in the field—
they tried to escape again, shooting
justified—so we devised a way
we couldn't be sent to work
in the cane or the cotton.

It didn't hurt much, just a little sting,
but when that tendon let loose
and flew up your leg,
you could sure feel that.

After the warden came to tell us
he's got the big stick and nothing we do
will change anything, we sent out the word
and the next day what do we see
but a parade of Heel-Slashers limping in, hollering
about no more fourteen-hour days, no more whippings
because they can't keep up in the big line,
no more flogging for taking a piss.

And so it became something else,
something bigger. In spite of ourselves
we turned this swamp hole inside out
all the way to the governor's mansion
and even though I been out and back in,
made out to be the hero I'm not,
that little catch in my step reminds me
I done something I'm proud of.

WILLIAM RICHARDSON READING *HAMLET* IN CHARITY HOSPITAL, NEW ORLEANS

When I severed my Achilles tendon
I thought I was making a stab "to be" rather than "not to be,"
getting myself into the hospital and away from
the unpredictable meanness of my boss, kennel guard
 Sergeant Perkins,
and the more predictable meanness of my fellow inmates.

But to be in prison is not that simple.
Sergeant Perkins barged right past Nurse Daughtry and pulled out
 a gun:
I've got your walking papers right here when you get well.
Then Foreman Manuel paid a visit:
I'm going to put you on Point Lookout and save the state money.
The first day I hobbled off the ward, Captain Melder continued
 this scene:
When this episode is over, I'm going to see that you cut your throat.

The croaking ravens are bellowing for revenge.
Lucky for me, my appendix was ready to burst
and they rushed me to Charity Hospital
where I could call my lawyer.
Judge Kilbourne granted me a temporary injunction,
a kind of restraining order to keep their hands off me.

I'm twenty-two, ten months left on my eighteen-month sentence
for trying to buy an ounce of marijuana—which by the way
is easier to get in prison than out.
*I didn't know if I was going to wind up stick-simple
from getting beat on, or scalped, like some I saw,
or dead. What good would a parole do then?*

              Remaking Achilles

STUNT MAN: GOVERNOR EARL LONG

I've been to Angola twice in the last two weeks
to investigate these allegations.

*It was my observation that
there is less brutality than there has ever been.
There was nothing to it.* Conditions are *better
than they have been in years.*

Cane and corn production are higher than any other time in
    Angola's history
and in the last three years cattle production has jumped 150%.
We've spent the money from my predecessor's allocations
wisely: two churches, a movie theater, a new hospital.

This is a publicity stunt, inmates claiming they can get anyone
they want fired. We need to maintain order, discipline.
I'd like to send a psychiatrist from the lunatic asylum
to find out what's in the minds of these Heel-Slashers.
Craziness.

WARDEN EASTERLY TALKS TO THE PRESS

All this publicity for these Heel-Stringers
makes me want to go on a slashing spree.
Some prisoners have bragged they can get
any official removed they want
but they've got one fellow who's not going to chunk—
they're not going to push me around.
Camp E where this all started is full of *degenerates*
and they are not going to run this prison.
This is a plot to wreck prison discipline
and force my removal.

The press has no idea what it takes
to manage an 18,000 acre farm
with this motley work force.
I like to farm and they don't
but they are not going to sit on their sorry asses
and expect the state of Louisiana to feed them.
I don't care if they have to crawl
to the field, they are going to work
and work hard.

BEFORE I WAS ACHILLES II

They want to brand us a bunch of psychopaths
and degenerates so they can dismiss what we done
as crazy. I may be homosexual, but I don't
beat men for a living, drown them in castor oil,
steal meat off their plates.

When I heard what Wallace and them done
I felt a jolt inside, a big whoop.
First thing I wanted to do in a long time.

Felt like communion—pass me that razor
let that blood be shed, break this body
so the world will know we are men
even if we be broken.

We hop to the hospital window—
men look up, we give a little dance.
When those reporters bust in weeks later
we still riding that high.

TAKING THE LONG VIEW: SUPERINTENDENT LAWRENCE

I know Governor Long thinks I'm too soft on inmates
too kind and too considerate
and he was pleased as punch when the legislature voted
to have a superintendent *and* a warden six months ago
so he could appoint someone he considers tougher.

But I think Warden Easterly's done a credible job,
even if we sometimes clash.
I interviewed those Heel-Stringers myself
and found evidence of only two cases of being hit
and that was done by the guards in self-defense.

As for the allegations of brutality,
I ordered the stocks removed from Camp A and as far as
those press reports about whippings in the Negro camps
*this is the first I heard of it. In Easterly's time as warden
I've had no brutality presented to me
either verbally or in writing.*

LUNCH WITH THE WARDEN:
E.M. CLINTON, REPORTER *TIMES-PICAYUNE*

We might have been at a fancy restaurant in Baton Rouge
or guests at a prosperous plantation: the artfully arranged
napkins, the salad and dessert forks, the goblets,
our inmate waiters attentive to our every need,
our host, Warden Easterly, eager to talk about
this year's cotton crop or his plans for the sugar refinery.
We looked out from the veranda at the spring green
lulled by the lushness of the land.

After lunch the warden brought in a tray of weapons—
files ground to knives, a toothbrush honed to sharpness—
the result of a shakedown that morning.
"Don't be fooled by this idyllic setting.
These prisoners are murderers and rapists, up to no good.
We've got to be vigilant."

When we asked about the Heel-Stringers
he waved his hand dismissively:
Malingerers, just didn't want to work
so they figured a way to get in the hospital
and off the duty list. He swiped his mouth
with a napkin as if to say end of meal, end of story.

We pressed for details: When did the heel slashings start?
How many? How did the staff respond?
What about the allegations of brutality?
We wanted a shakedown of the truth.

In an office a string of warden-selected inmates testified
how these reports of brutality were exaggerated,
publicity seekers. No one had complaints.

Stories leaked out from men we interviewed outside the office:
beatings, forced castor oil, handcuffed to a bedpost overnight
    standing,
the relentless goading to work faster.

By the time we insisted on visiting the hospital
to talk with the Heel-Stringers themselves, the shakedown of truth
had shaken us. We hobbled out of Angola.

The warden knew what had happened:
he had opened the gates too wide.
The next morning, when Ed Stagg from *The Item*
tried to get in, he was told the press was barred,
which made us more determined to get in.
We had gotten a whiff of Angola
and we weren't stopping.

SECOND CUT

Word has it we Heel Street Boogie Boys
were being sent back to Camp E and we know
after all we done told those reporters
Camp E a death sentence so we go for
the right leg this time, nothing else left.

Warden can't believe we still got a blade
after all that shakedown. Make us laugh inside
hear him cussing at the guards, threaten them
with Old Hickory Stick.

Warden say we heard those reporters coming back
and we *wanted to put on another show.*
Only show we care about is staying alive.
Can't do the Heel Street Boogie no more
but we hear it in our heads and know
we still here, dancing.

DISCOVERING THE DUNGEONS: EDWARD W. STAGG, CAPITOL CORRESPONDENT NEW ORLEANS *ITEM*

*Angola is a telling example of man's habit of trying to get rid of
problems by forgetting them. —Edward Stagg*

The story broke in *The Shreveport Journal* on Saturday, Feb. 24
with an anonymous tip-off from a prisoner who had been released:
thirty-one prisoners had slashed their Achilles tendons.

On Monday I headed out to Angola unannounced.
It took some wrangling—Warden Easterly had banned press entry
and it took calls to the governor from my editor—
but I finally made it through the gate. Everyone was on edge.
The guards who checked my car took twice as long,
more guards on horseback than I had ever seen,
more traffic, tunnels of dust crisscrossing.

I walked into the hospital and saw a procession
of limping men, blood streaming down their legs:
ten Heel-Slashers had just cut their right heel
now that the left ones were mending.

Later, when I was part of the investigating committee,
we stumbled on what looked like a solid block of concrete
with three iron pipes stuck up like periscopes.
We clambered over it like a shipwreck
trying to figure out what it was.

When we found an unlocked door
we peered into darkness—walls and ceiling black,
no windows, barely enough room to stand,
the air thick and rotted.

Even after we drove back to Baton Rouge
I couldn't get that smell out of my head.
I was gagging on Angola.

At the hearing Warden Easterly still insisted
there was no justification for the heel slashings.
That made me gag, too.

INSIDE THE BIG HOUSE:
THE CITIZEN COMMITTEE INVESTIGATION

FEBRUARY TO APRIL, 1951

WILBER BLACKIE COMEAUX TALKS TO REPORTERS

Yes, I'm a third-time offender—
ten months the last round—
and it's the worst I've seen it since '40
a place that ain't fit for hogs,
sexual perverts operating in the open
free people takin' the meat and leaving
bones and scraps for us cons,
packages from home stolen.

You want to know about beatings?
Go to the hospital and ask for Walter Ott
and Angelo Stafford. They might not talk—
after a prisoner talked to your committee
he got *kicked around like a football*—
but you can see for yourself.

Warden say you reporters bringing
all these fantastic stories about Angola—if you don't quit,
there's gonna be some lawsuits. Ought a be a lawsuit
against him all those lies he's telling to cover his butt.
Those Heel-Slashers done slit Angola open.
I would a done it, too, if I was still in The Big House.

FOUND POEM 3: "MARSE" CLIFFORD LEAKE ADDRESSES THE COMMITTEE ON DAY 1

I never cussed prisoners—it's against the warden's rules.
I speak to them like a man.
I never lost my temper and hit any of them.
I never had a prisoner resist me.
I'm only a foreman.
It would be against the rules for me to punish a prisoner.
I report them to the captain and he takes care of the punishment.

NURSE DAUGHTRY CROSSES THE RUBICON

When Warden Easterly came to my home
I knew the shit was hitting the fan.

Before he could say a word, I told him
he didn't have to call me to testify.

The committee will want to hear from you.

I looked down at my clasped hands.

There's nothing wrong here.

I looked up, met his glare eye to eye.

Name your price, you'll have a job for life.

I thought about my husband, the hospital captain.
We lived here, this was our life.

I told him I'd think it over.

When he left, I walked to the hospital
and headed for the Heel-Slashers ward.

All the injuries I had seen over my seven years at Angola
seemed to rise up from that row of beds.

I went to my office and started typing.
I didn't stop until morning.

TRUTH OR CONSEQUENCES: DOLPH FRANTZ, EDITOR *SHREVEPORT JOURNAL*, CHAIR INVESTIGATION COMMITTEE

Our first two days of hearings were like a dream,
prisoners and guards and administrators streaming
in and out and we had no idea how they had been chosen.
Why had thirty-seven men slashed their Achilles tendons?
Laziness, homosexual jealousy, push out the new Camp E Captain,
push out Warden Easterly?

The field foreman Heel-Slashers named
as the most brutal, Clifford Leake,
insisted that in his twenty-two years as a guard
he had never hit a prisoner, or even cussed one.

What was true and what wasn't?
After two days of testimony, E.M. Clinton
of *The Times-Picayune* got it right:
little if anything was proved except that
somebody is not telling the truth.

By the end of the second day, as the light
through the chapel windows faded, my head ached.
Then the lady several inmates had named
as a key witness, Nurse Mary Margaret Daughtry,
walked in and quietly handed us four typewritten pages.
From that moment we started to find our footing.

FOUND POEM 4: NURSE DAUGHTRY'S
STATEMENT TO THE COMMITTEE

No one has ever asked me if I have seen evidence of brutality
but I have seen plenty. Angola is still in the Dark Ages.
Sex offenders, stool pigeons, homosexuals,
degenerates of every type, psychopaths and neurotics,
are huddled in huge dormitories that, as one inmate described to me,
stink like the hold of a slave ship.

There is no trade school, no handicrafts or arts—not even a library.
A man sentenced here who cannot read or write
leaves here the same way.
No effort is made to help him stay out
of the penitentiary once he obtains his release.
I do not believe the Heel-String cutters mutilated themselves
simply to escape being whipped or beaten. These acts
were the culmination of many things joined together
to destroy their morale and warp their minds.

Governor Long said the penitentiary has been a cancer
on the state treasury. I say that the penitentiary
is a cancer on the soul of every citizen in the state of Louisiana
who knows of conditions at Angola
and has made no effort to remedy them.

DECKED OUT: MAGGIE DIXON, EDITOR BATON ROUGE *MORNING ADVOCATE*, VICE-CHAIR INVESTIGATION COMMITTEE

I wasn't trying to upstage the investigation
but when Sheriff Martin started throwing
his weight around, threatening to arrest Nurse Daughtry
for possession of heroin that she bought to show us
just how easy it is get drugs at Angola, I insisted
on taking possession of those two decks myself.
I've been in Louisiana politics long enough
to know intimidation when I see it.
We had promised immunity to all our witnesses
and I was going to uphold that promise.
Let that cottonpickin' sheriff come after me.
If he doesn't back off, I'll put in print
every ridiculous word he says.

DOUBLE DECKER: SHERIFF TEDDY MARTIN

Maggie Dixon, I can't believe you won't turn over
the heroin you got from Nurse Daughtry.
Governor Long appointed me as secretary
of this investigation committee but I can't do my job
as sheriff of West Feliciana Parish if you won't comply
with my order. Just because you're the vice-chair
doesn't mean you are above the law
and Nurse Daughtry isn't either.
I'm going to prosecute her and whoever
sold it to her, I don't care if people were promised
immunity if they testified. Possession of heroin is a felony.
When they say the *Morning Advocate* is the paper of
convicts and crazies, they're right.
A bunch of hooey—that's what I call this whole hullabaloo.
The trouble with these fellows is they can't get away anymore
and they'll do anything to keep from working
and apparently you will do anything to wave a red flag
in front of your readers to rile them up.
Stop protecting criminals and hand over that contraband.

WARDEN EASTERLY RESPONDS
TO NURSE DAUGHTRY'S TESTIMONY

I've got deep pockets, so I thought
I could get everyone inside them.
That damn nurse. Every year I read
her report—so capable, so confident—
no need for a doctor with a high salary when
we had Nurse Daughtry.

I put up with her syphilis treatments
and her constant complaining about
the lack of medical facilities,
gave her just about every damn thing
she wanted, including a new hospital.

Now she's on a high horse, thinks
she can rehabilitate these degenerates.
She's a woman, thinks a soft touch
will turn things around. She doesn't understand
what you have to do to prevent chaos
from sweeping in.

I should put her in charge and let her see
how you have to rule with a heavy hand.

ACHILLES RESPONDS TO NURSE DAUGHTRY'S TESTIMONY: BEFORE I WAS ACHILLES III

When we heard about Nurse Daughtry
letting it rip to that investigation committee
we did our Heel Street Boogie again.
If they didn't trust our word, we thought
here's somebody they might believe.

We knew she had seen the worst—
men with arms broken by guards,
men so weak from days in the dungeon
they couldn't walk, men whose backs
Old Hickory Stick had broken, men with asses
torn to pieces from forced sex, men who died
from sunstroke, men with heart failure from taking bennies
to survive the long line.

The day after she gave her testimony
she was gone—we never had the chance to thank her.
Over my bed I taped a picture of a big green hill in Ireland
and every night I looked at that Irish April
and said her name.

WARDEN EASTERLY TESTIFIES
TO THE INVESTIGATION COMMITTEE

You know who's behind these heel slashings?
At first I thought it was the prisoners who wanted
to get rid of me—I make them work—but now I realize it's
Nurse Daughtry. *She did this so she can get rid of me*
and the prison doctor, too. She got rid of other people—
she's after me.

You heard Sheriff Martin say he's going to report
her *to the State Medical Association for illegally*
practicing medicine in the parish. I second that.

FOUND POEM 5: PICAYUNES

Maybe that heel-slashing at Angola means someone is not on his toes.
—Peter Baird, *Times-Picayune*, February 28, 1951

In charges of sordid conditions at the Angola prison there are more
pros than cons. —Peter Baird, *Times-Picayune*, March 16, 1951

CLIFFORD LACOSTE TAKES OFF THE RED HAT

I wasn't trying to make a statement
like those Heel-Stringers I met in the hospital.
I even asked to be moved to the Red Hat
when they released me from the ward.
The barracks were too much, 300 men in one room,
had to be on guard every minute and I didn't have the energy
after lying in bed a couple days.

Doc they brought in said my heart was off kilter
even suspected it was bennies.
Sometimes I just needed one to keep
the pace in the field and not get whipped.
Got out of hand, hadn't slept in three days.

Coroner couldn't say I overdosed
all the hubbub with Nurse Daughtry
trying to show that committee how dope
gets around here. Suicide by hanging instead.

I hear via the prison grapevine my death
is part of the Heel-String investigation.
A woman on the committee, Nona Martin—
damn I hate to miss her visit—came to Camp E
and talked to everyone who knew me,
then called for an investigation into my death.

I never did much good in my life.
There's a chance my death can change that,
even if by accident.

EASTER UPRISING: HAMILTON ISRAEL

Don't know exactly what happened,
one minute we was eatin' breakfast—
food measly like always, but at least
we not in the field today—
next minute like a volcano
go off—500 black men
throwin' bread and spoons and plates.

We used to mindin' our own business,
complainin' get yourself whipped—
none of us Negroes done that heel-slashing—
but last Wednesday, when that committee
come to Camp A, we hear ourselves
bustin' loose—beatings by hose pipe papa,
stocks that break your back,
Willie and Charles and Henry droppin' their pants
to show them black grooves.

We got called the ringleaders of this "riot."
We the ones spoke up, tell Judge Spaht
it's as bad here as at Camp E or worse,
at least 40 men here have hose pipe marks
they'll carry to their graves—we all know
that rubber hose he use, thinkin' it won't
leave no signs on black flesh.

Warden come bustin' in, expect us to listen.
There's no stoppin' us, *you SOB,* we yell at Easterly.
Somebody run in the kitchen, grab a meat cleaver,
warden run right out with the guards.

Inside the Big House

We know we gonna pay later—
the sweatbox waitin' for us, Easter reversed—
but right now we done astonished ourselves,
let the truth explode.

SHERIFF MARTIN CELEBRATES EASTER, 1951

How many times do I have to say that damn investigation
is putting everyone in West Feliciana Parish in danger.
I've been sheriff here for 18 years and this place is a keg of dynamite—
anytime anybody tried to pet and pamper these people, there was trouble.
All this jabbering about brutality, Captains can't do their jobs.
These men aren't here for ringing church bells.

Now I got to leave my Easter brunch and rush all the way out here
    with my deputies—
ruin their Easter, too—and clamp the lid on a box that never should
    of been opened.
I've heard Warden Easterly say *we've lost some guns up there.*
I'm afraid we're going to be looking at them before many moons.
Thank God all they had was meat cleavers.

Soon as they saw those submachine guns they stopped this nonsense.
I rounded up the ringleaders—the guards told me who had been
    blabbin'
to that sub-committee chair, Judge Spaht—tossed them in the
    dungeon.
Next thing you know they'll be sayin' solitary is cruel and unusual
    punishment.
As far as I'm concerned, that's where the whole damn committee
    ought to be.

Inside the Big House

A FESTER ON THE FACE OF DEMOCRACY: DOLPH FRANTZ, EDITOR *SHREVEPORT JOURNAL*, CHAIR INVESTIGATION COMMITTEE

We released our report April 20, the same day General MacArthur
proclaimed
to Congress, *An old soldier never dies, he just fades away.*
Angola prisoners die and fade away
and it was our job not to let that happen.

At the end of the sixty days Governor Long gave us
we didn't have all the answers, but we had a reasonably clear
understanding:
the beatings were a reality. Besides the evidence written on
inmate bodies,
prison files included reprimands for excessive violence
from Superintendent Lawrence, including one on Clifford Leake.
But beatings were the tip of the iceberg—gambling rings, drug
trafficking,
sexual assaults, sweat boxes, favors for cash, bribes for pardons,
horrible sanitation—
a fester on the face of democracy.

We came up with a list of twenty recommendations, what to add,
what to subtract:
hire a trained warden, address sanitation and medical care,
develop recreation and education, separate first-time offenders, build
new housing;
get rid of corporal punishment, inmate guards, the dungeons,
which just about adds up to what one committee member told
the governor—
What it boils down to is tear the place down and start over.

The response of those in power was swift:
the press was barred from Angola, claiming those in charge
should be left alone to carry out the recommendations.
Superintendent Lawrence got the boot and instead of hiring a
     trained warden
Governor Earl Long gave Warden Easterly total authority.

It would be another year before anything changed,
when conditions at Angola rumbled the governor race.
Long after his defeat, the incorrigible Earl said,
I thought the committee would vindicate me,
but it hanged me instead.
Prisoners at Angola had been hung out for years.

OF, FOR, AND BY THE PEOPLE: GOVERNOR EARL LONG

As governor, it is my responsibility to sort through
these recommendations and figure out what's common sense
and what's nonsense. All this squawkin' 'bout hiring some outsider
who learned about prison in schoolbooks.
This is a Louisiana prison, paid for by the citizens
of Louisiana—of, for and by the people of Louisiana—
and just because another state hires trained
prison administrators doesn't mean that's what's right
for Louisiana, no need to be copycattin'.
Warden Easterly is *thoroughly capable—everything he does*
is successful and we were fortunate to get him,
and that recommendation for a rehabilitation program?
You want us to teach those convicts ping-pong,
baseball, elocution and gee-tar playin'?
We got a farm to run and before I leave this office
this prison is going to be financially solvent,
not *a cancer on state finances.*
That's the work we've got to do.

AFTERMATH: AIN'T OVER YET

BEYOND APRIL, 1951

WARDEN EASTERLY REFUSES TO MEET THE PRESS

You tell those reporters *I've been nice to you*
and all you've done is cause me trouble. They have been running
all around the place for the past sixty days, and *my God*
they write up everything a rotten old inmate says
and as for that testimony by Nurse Daughtry
you can *put my record against hers any day.*
The governor's done with that damn citizen committee.
Your work's finished and your report is sitting on my desk
where it will get buried under all the work it takes
to keep this prison from falling further to the dogs.
Superintendent Lawrence is gone and I'm calling the shots.
These people printing all these fantastic stories about Angola—
if they don't quit, there's going to be some lawsuits.
Go home and stay there because you are not setting foot in here
unless you've got a prison ID number.

Aftermath: Ain't Over Yet

MAGGIE'S PIPELINE

Maggie's at her desk when the call comes in.
"Mike," she asks me as I'm walking by,
"what kind of beer do you drink?"
I tell her Jax, wondering if she's planning a party for me
making it through my first year as a city reporter covering
the NAACP without getting killed.
"Jax," she says and hangs up.

"Something's gone wrong at Angola,"
she tells me with that fierce glare that I'm glad
she never turns on me.
"Head out to that bar near Standard Oil
and order a beer."

I'm sipping my Jax when a guy without teeth
asks me to join his buddies at the back.
Three just-released inmates report
the breaking of a baseball bat
on a prisoner's head by the warden.

I rush back to the newsroom.
Maggie sends another reporter to Angola
so the story can't be traced.
The warden denies the story
until Bill points out the bloody bat
leaning against the wall behind the desk.

If something's going down at Angola,
Maggie will find out.

DUNGEONS AT ANGOLA DESTROYED BY KENNON AS PRISONERS WATCH

That's the headline I wrote September 24, 1952
for the *Morning Advocate*. Over a year had passed
since we finished our investigation of the Heel-Stringers
and finally something was happening,
one of our recommendations put into action
right there in front of us.

The new governor, Robert Kennon,
and the new warden, Sam Anderson,
drove that bulldozer straight at that hell-hole
and in two pushes it was over.

It was a staged event—reporters scribbling,
photographers snapping, legislators nodding—
but the real event happened behind us,
outside the Camp A dorm where the prisoners watched,
their bodies black against the whitewashed wall.

They whooped and hollered as if it were a boxing match—
get him, take him down—as if all those years
someone had them by the throat and now
they were back on their feet, swaying and clapping
and no one was ever going to bury them alive again.

Aftermath: Ain't Over Yet

THE HOLE TRUTH

I done spent four days in The Hole last summer—
couldn't tell day from night, walls and ceiling
painted black, no windows,
like you dead, buried in a box.

Ain't no accident The Hole in Camp A
black men buried in blackness
a concrete box for a toilet
only bread and water pushed through a slot
once a day—if you're lucky—
the smell of your piss and shit
roastin' in that oven and

on top that two-inch pipe
a blade of air so you don't suffocate—
only the time they threw eight of us in
seven crawled out.

Glad that dungeon gone—
want to believe it's done, but I seen my daddy
in that sweat box called sharecroppin'
and I know it ain't over yet.

TENDING: MAGGIE DIXON, MANAGING EDITOR
BATON ROUGE *MORNING ADVOCATE*, 1949–1970

I grew up taking care of people,
first my stepsisters, because my mother had TB
and then a long line of reporters who needed tending.

In the forties, the men were the leftovers
the ones who couldn't serve
and they felt their inadequacies keenly—
they needed bolstering.

The women were breaking ground
pushing out of the society pages to cover
murders, scandals, racial tensions—
they needed cheering.

I have the Manships to thank
for sticking with the women after the war ended,
nearly half the staff female by then.

In 1948 *Newsweek* headlined a story on the *Advocate*
"The Women." I would have preferred "The Newsmen"
and let the photo speak for itself—Managing Editor,
City Editor, and Telegraph Editor wearing dresses.

In my life as a journalist I had two pinpoints—politics and prison—
but I always *cared more about the people than the news.*

LETTERS TO MAGGIE DIXON

On the subject of Angola, Maggie was this state's conscience.
—Elayn Hunt

After the investigation, when the press was barred from Angola,
letters would appear stuck in the carriage of my typewriter
in the hours after the paper went to press.

A father pleading for mental health services for a son at Angola.
An inmate seeking help finding work, necessary before parole
would even be considered. A priest who spent only a week at Angola
begging me to continue advocating for more humane conditions—
of all the people in Louisiana, I feel that you will understand.

A mother—*My son has been in Angola almost 16 months,*
he is serving time for a crime he didn't commit.
I was told to write you for help.
A group of inmates on a hunger strike—
This entire prison is a cesspool of corruption.

A prisoner pleading to have his wife re-instated onto his visitor list.
An invitation to visit and hear firsthand an account of brutality—
we are protesting to get one free man removed, who is doing the beating.
A plea to give news coverage to an accusation of brutality
so a prisoner will not receive retaliation.

A request to edit a clemency plea—*I worry it's too long-winded.*
An inmate requesting I check on the delivery of his *Morning Advocate*
that fails to arrive some mornings.

I both treasured and dreaded these letters
always asking for more than I could do,
always driving me to do what I could.

CONFESSION: CAMILLUS ELLSPERMANN, OSB, WRITING TO MAGGIE DIXON

I am availing myself of the invitation to write to you personally
because of all the people in Louisiana, I feel that you will understand.
I ask myself frequently if my personal involvement was complete enough
in the very disturbing events that took place during my replacement
of the chaplain. I was only at Angola one week, but
what saddened and moved me was to see a system
that could permit human beings treated like animals.

I know you have heard this before, but I have to tell someone.
The hours of my office, when I should be praying,
are filled with horrific scenes: beatings, vulgar language,
lack of sanitary facilities—sometimes not even allowed a toilet,
for God's sake—graft and petty cruelties like arbitrarily changing
a prisoner's visiting or mail list. How can I sit here in my
    comfortable cell
when I know the utter disregard for human life
I have witnessed?

I have given my testimony to the F.B.I., trying to name
only what I saw and not what inmates told me, as I was instructed,
although that troubles me, too, as I heard so much more.

I much appreciated the clippings you sent me
and hope to hear more about what might be done
to bring basic human decency to this earthly Hell.

Aftermath: Ain't Over Yet

PAROLEE

Every morning I thank God I was paroled
a week before the funeral of Maggie Dixon.
When I hobbled into St. James
I felt like I was paying my respects to one of the saints.

I only met her once, the day I testified
to that committee after we done slashed our heels,
but I remember how she listened
like a bell be ringing in her head.
From that day on I read the *Morning Advocate*
every day, knowing I was gonna see something
'bout what was going on at Angola.

After the investigation of us Heel-Stringers
she kept up the pressure, every day
writing about all those recommendations
and nothing happening—no library, no job training,
same trustee guards, same hickory stick
even if the governor say it was banned

and when Warden Easterly threw the press out
she fought to get back in,
throwing the law in Governor Long's face
how it's illegal to deny anyone with legitimate business
entry into Angola.

When she was allowed back in—
though still no talking to us inmates—
we found a way to get the word to her.
We're out in the sticks, but for Maggie it's like
we was always close by, like we be neighbors.

420 ACRE DAY

Rain beyond rain, too wet to work fields.
I play cards, rub the scar on my heel.
At dinner the Captain growling about time wasted,
cotton popping, money lost.

Late Saturday I look up from my sorry hand
and see the sun burning all that cotton
and me smirking because tomorrow's Sunday—
our one day of rest.

The warden come in our camp begging
talking 'bout chicken dinners,
soft drinks, Monday off,
sleep late, steak for breakfast.

Steak. What I want can't be eaten—
fill a thousand sacks with the days I got left,
pile them on a truck, drive out the gate,
take all the Heel-Stringers still alive with me.

That would be a 420 acre day.

RED HAT REDUX: REMEMBERING CLIFFORD LACOSTE

They come to me when they were restoring Red Hat
cuz I can cut a straight line with my brush, no tape.
After fifty years, I got a steady hand—
a miracle I'm still here—five or six years here
and most dead.

I never set foot inside Red Hat and I want to see
the cell where my buddy Clifford hung hisself in 51—
or that's what they told us—who knows what
really happened. Clifford, he tough, tried to escape
twice. Can't imagine he give up.
Told that to Nona Martin when they investigating.

Now folks coming on cruise ships
down the Mississippi to see the Red Hat
as an Historic Landmark, see those concrete beds
and puny windows without screens, read those
signs about prisoners beaten with the bat
or ten men stuffed in one cell.

I painted that red trim for tourists so they know
they're at Red Hat—plain white with a green door before—
used to put a red stripe on the straw hat of anyone
from this block so guards keep an extra eye on 'em.
Wish I had Clifford's hat—if he had one—
only at Red Hat one day.

Hard to believe tourists come all the way to Angola
to see where Charles Frazier—that bank robber
nobody could keep locked in—lived his last seven years,
his Red Hat cell door welded shut.
No sign for Clifford.

Still, I think it be good his ghost
get some company, especially them
women in their slinky dresses.
Used to spook me, hurry by Red Hat
all those spirits hovering at the window,
Gruesome Gertie just waiting for a body
when they start using the chair here,
but I ain't so scared now—kind of proud—
I paint that red line for you, Clifford Lacoste,
so your last home look real good.

POINT LOOKOUT: BECOMING ACHILLES

Some inmates want to be buried here
want that ride up to Lookout in that fancy hearse
look like a stagecoach pulled by horses
and some make it known they want out
even if it's wrapped in cardboard, though nowadays
after a body fell right out of a wet box
they got this woodshop turns out a first-class coffin.

Me, after my heel got infected, wasn't even allowed
into Lookout, no white cross in a white picket fence.
I got shipped to New Orleans in a body bag
smelling like shit bad as that castor oil day.
Those researchers went at me with their
razor-sharp knives that I envied. It would have hurt
a whole lot less with a blade like that. When they got
to my heel, oozing with poison, they named me
Achilles. Best name I ever been called.

NOTES

Lines in italics are taken directly from primary sources.

THE LEASED OF THESE

These poems are informed by Mark Carleton's *Politics and Punishment: The History of the Louisiana State Penal System*, materials from the Angola Museum, and the article "Plantation Prisons" by Marianne Fisher-Giorlando.

"First Heel Slashing": The story of Theophile Chevalier was reported by an investigative committee of the Louisiana General Assembly in 1886. The committee visited several of the work camps to which prisoners were leased. Any actions taken by the committee in response are undocumented.

"Leasee": The italicized lines come from S.L. James' obituary, *Daily Picayune* July 28, 1894.

THE LONG LINE

A number of poems in this section use material from a series of essays, "Hell on Angola," published in the New Orleans *Item* in 1943. Written by William Sadler, known as Wooden Ear due to a hearing loss from a prison attack, the series gives readers a prisoner's view of Angola in the late thirties and early forties. Sadler published an in-house newspaper, the *Argus*, during his first prison term (1935–1943). Returning to Angola in the early fifties, Sadler became the first editor of *The Angolite*, which became an award-winning prison news magazine. The "Hell on Angola" series, now available through the Angola Museum website, was unearthed from the Tulane University archives by Angola historian Marianne Fisher-Giorlando.

"It Bad Enough": The inmate comment "stink like the hold of a slave ship" comes directly from the testimony of Nurse Daughtry, who submitted a 4-page report to the citizen committee.

"Fifties Photo": This photo, taken by Wilfred D'Aquin, accompanied the article "America's Worst Prison" by Edward W. Stagg and John Lear in the November 22, 1952 *Collier's Magazine*. Stagg, a reporter for the New Orleans *Item*, was part of the citizen committee that investigated the Heel-String incident.

"Convict Guards": The "Hell on Angola" series, as well as a report titled "The Inmate Guard" by Jack Wright, Jr., Assistant Professor of Criminology, Florida State, document the use of inmates as guards. Wright bitingly sums up the convict guard system: "Thus Louisiana finds itself in the position of saving money by having its inmates guarded by borderline retards, the majority of whom have been convicted of a crime of violence."

REMAKING ACHILLES

The poems in this section are informed by local newspaper articles that followed the story of the Heel-Stringers.

"Lineage": Philip Verheyen, son of a subsistence farmer from a small Flemish village, trained for the priesthood until a severe infection led to gangrene and subsequently a leg amputation. This turned Verheyen toward the study of medicine. Instructed by the highly recognized Dutch anatomists of the day, Verheyen, who became a professor of anatomy, authored an anatomy textbook that was widely used for fifty years. While the story of his own leg dissection may be apocryphal, it is well documented that Verheyen coined the term Achilles tendon.

"Heel Street Boogie": In 1948 Tommy Sargent and the Range Boys recorded "Steel Guitar Boogie." The Baton Rouge *State Times* Feb. 27, 1951 reports that the Heel-Stringers wrote a parody of this tune and named it "Heel Street Boogie."

"Tunnel-Digger to Heel-Stringer": Wallace MacDonald was the last surviving Heel-Stringer. Anne Butler and C. Murray Henderson interviewed MacDonald for the book *Angola Louisiana State Penitentiary: A Half-Century of Rage and Reform*.

"William Richardson: Reading *Hamlet*": The Baton Rouge *State Times* June 6, 1951 and the Baton Rouge *Morning Advocate* June 7 and June 30, 1951 reported William Richardson's unusual request for a restraining order for prison staff. Eventually the injunction was denied because the Angola employees in question claimed they had never beaten Richardson. After he recuperated from his surgery, Richardson was sent back to prison. The articles also noted that Richardson was reading a volume of Shakespeare while he recuperated.

"Discovering the Dungeons": Edward Stagg, co-author of the *Collier's* article "America's Worst Prison," describes the dungeons: "The entire cubicle was the size of a small clothes closet. Into this stifling space as many as seven men were jammed at a time. At least one man had been removed in a state just short of roasting."

INSIDE THE BIG HOUSE

Again, local newspaper articles proved an invaluable source for understanding the twists and turns of the investigation.

"Found Poem 3: 'Marse' Clifford Leake Addresses the Committee on Day 1": At the time of the Heel-Slashing incident, Clifford Leake had worked at Angola for over twenty-two years, from 1920 on with a hiatus between 1940–1948. As a field foreman, he supervised 60–80 men. A number of Heel-Stringers singled out Leake as one of the most brutal guards. Baton Rouge *Morning Advocate* March 8 and *Times-Picayune* March 8.

"Found Poem 4: Nurse Daughtry's Statement to the Committee": Excerpts from Nurse Daughtry's testimony appeared in *Collier's Magazine* Nov. 22, 1952. An additional account of Nurse Daughtry's testimony comes from the March 9, 1951 Baton Rouge *Morning Advocate*.

"Decked Out": Eventually a local judge ordered the heroin turned over to the court and Maggie Dixon complied.

"Clifford LaCoste Takes Off the Red Hat": Clifford LaCoste was found dead in the Red Hat cellblock a few weeks after the heel slashings. While the death was officially named a suicide, there were enough uncertainties around the circumstances that committee member Nona Martin, who was in charge of the sub-committee on prison facilities and general care of prisoners, called for an investigation of LaCoste's death. The Red Hat Cellblock was the first structure that kept prisoners in individual cells at Angola. Built after Charles Frazier's notorious escape in 1933, the Red Hat cell block housed up to thirty high-risk prisoners that wore hats with a swipe of red paint so they could be easily identified when they worked in the fields.

AFTERMATH: AIN'T OVER YET

Along with newspaper and magazine articles, the papers of Maggie Dixon, housed in the Special Collection at Louisiana State University, and John DeMers' M.A. thesis, *Maggie: The Life and Times of the Louisiana Newspaper Woman*, contributed greatly to my understanding of the role Maggie Dixon played at Angola. Three facilities named after Dixon—a visitor's center at Angola, a correctional institute at Jackson, and an outpatient unit for children—pay tribute to her lifelong concern for those in the grip of the criminal justice system.

"Letters to Maggie Dixon": Elayn Hunt, author of the epigraph, was one of the female reporters Maggie Dixon encouraged. Hunt, a crime reporter for the Baton Rouge *State Times*, and Dixon made frequent trips together to Angola. Hunt went on to pursue a career as a criminal defense lawyer and eventually directed the Department of Corrections in Louisiana from 1972–76, a controversial appointment due to her gender. Under her leadership, the inmate guards at Angola were replaced with professionals and the Red Hat cellblock was closed. She also worked for better food, drug treatment programs and other rehabilitation services.

"Confession": Although the letter from Camillus Ellspermann, included in the papers of Maggie Dixon, is from 1965, in the midst of another investigation, I include it in this book for several reasons. Foremost, it continues to highlight the role Maggie Dixon played as a watch dog for Angola. The testimony from Camillus brings a different perspective, an outsider who has temporary access to the inside. His character also introduces theological questions: how do people of faith live out their religious convictions in the context of deep injustice?

"Red Hat Redux": The Red Hat unit closed in 1973. It was placed on the National Register of Historic Places in 2003. Inmates helped restore the unit, which first opened to visitors in 2012.

ACKNOWLEDGMENTS

The poem "Point Lookout: Becoming Achilles," in a slightly changed form, received an honorable mention in the 2016 Split This Rock poetry contest and appeared on their website.

My gratitudes:

To Marianne Fisher-Giorlando, Angola historian, who graciously shared her time and her documents

To the librarians at Mt. Mercy University for their ongoing patience with yet another request

To the Mt. Mercy Faculty Development Committee for funding my research and writing

To the staff at the Louisiana State University Special collections library for their kind assistance to a novice researcher

To Wilbert Rideau for his fierce writing on what happens inside prison and for introducing me to Angola history

To the men of the Anamosa State Penitentiary Book Club for letting me into their world

To my early readers—Andy Douglas, Cecile Goding, Mary Vermillion—for their encouragement and critique

To Barry, for helping me remember that big things happen in small steps

To Blue and Sam, who make it all worthwhile

CPSIA information can be obtained
at www.ICGtesting.com
Printed in the USA
LVHW091501181220
674449LV00015B/1497